The Costume Parade

The **first** costume is a clown.
What a funny clown!

The **second** costume is a ghost.
What a scary ghost!

The **third** costume is a butterfly.
What a pretty butterfly!

4

The **fourth** costume is a monster.
What an ugly monster!

5

The fifth costume is a bear.
What a fuzzy bear!

Who wins the prize?

"We all do!"

8